Slimy Snails

by Laura Hamilton Waxman

first step nonfiction

Lerner Publications ◆ Minneapolis

LERNER

SOURCE™

Expand learning beyond the printed book. Download free, complementary educational resources for this book from our website, www.lernerresource.com.

The images in this book are used with the permission of: © Rolf Nussbaumer Photography/Alamy, p. 4; © George Grall/National Geographic/Getty Images, p. 5; © Nikki O'Keefe Images/Moment Open/Getty Images, p. 6; © Spencer Grant/Photographer's Choice/Getty Images, p. 7; © Jerry & Nancy Monkman/ Animals Animals, p. 8; © Steve Byland/Dreamstime.com, p. 9; © Steeve Marcoux/Design Pics/Getty Images, p. 10; © DigitalVues/Alamy, p. 11; © Marvin Dembinsky Photo Associates/Alamy, p. 12; © MartinStr/ Pixabay, p. 13; © Doug Wechsler, p. 14; © Darlyne A. Murawski/National Geographic Magazine/Getty Images, p. 15; © Lourens Smak/Alamy, p. 16; © Francesco Tomasinelli/Science Source, p. 17; © Ko01/ Thinkstock, p. 18; © Ernie Janes/Alamy, p. 19; © Surendra Kumar Mali/EyeEm/Getty Images, p. 20; © Dwight Kuhn, p. 21; © Richard Shiell/Animals Animals, p. 22. Front cover: © jurra8/Shutterstock.com.

Main body text set in ITC Avant Garde Gothic Std Medium 21/25.
Typeface provided by International Typeface Corp.

Lerner Publications Company
A division of Lerner Publishing Group, Inc.
241 First Avenue North
Minneapolis, MN 55401 USA

For reading levels and more information, look up this title at www.lernerbooks.com.

Library of Congress Cataloging-in-Publication Data

Names: Waxman, Laura Hamilton, author.
Title: Slimy snails / by Laura Hamilton Waxman.
Description: Minneapolis : Lerner Publications, [2016] | Series: First step nonfiction. Backyard critters | Audience: Ages 5–8. | Audience: K to grade 3. | Includes index.
Identifiers: LCCN 2015037027| ISBN 9781512408799 (lb : alk. paper) | ISBN 9781512412222 (pb : alk. paper) | ISBN 9781512410037 (eb pdf)
Subjects: LCSH: Snails—Juvenile literature.
Classification: LCC QL430.4 .W393 2016 | DDC 594.3—dc23
LC record available at http://lccn.loc.gov/2015037027

Manufactured in the United States of America
1 – CG – 7/15/16

Table of Contents

Snail Bodies

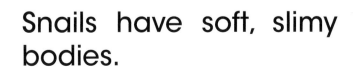

Snails have soft, slimy bodies.

They have hard, **spiral** shells.

This snail has two sets of feelers to help it find its way.

A snail's head is at one end of its body.

One long foot is under its shell.

Snail shells come in many shapes and sizes.

A snail can hide inside its shell.

Then it is safe from danger.

Where to Find Snails

Most snails live in **moist** places.

They will die if their bodies
dry out.

Many snails live in wet dirt
and leaves.

Snails can live in seas, ponds, or streams.

Other snails live in water.

Most snails eat plants and **algae**.

Other snails feed on small animals.

The food snails eat can be dead or alive.

A snail scrapes up food with tiny teeth.

The teeth are on its tongue.

What Snails Do

Snails make slime.

Slime keeps snails moist.

Snails also use slime to stick to things like glue.

Slime helps a snail move forward on its foot.

Follow the slime trail to
catch up to the snail!

Snail Parts

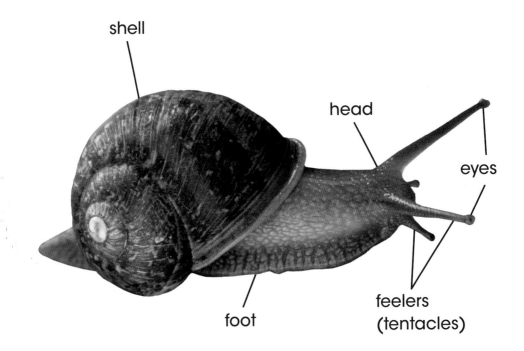

shell

head

eyes

foot

feelers
(tentacles)

Glossary

algae – plantlike living things that grow in nature

moist – a little wet

spiral – circling around a center spot

Index